The Story
of David Livingstone

by

Vautier Golding

·

Contents

EARLY LIFE

THE story of this brave and gentle hero, and of his noble toil for the sake of other men, is truly a tale of more than ordinary wonder.

Few men's lives can better show how even the poorest and weakest can gain for themselves the power to do great things, and to make the harder paths of life more easy for those who follow. For David Livingstone began life in a workman's cottage, without knowledge or skill, and without money to obtain them. Yet, when he died, the world was so full of praise and wonder at his work that his body was brought from Africa to rest in Westminster Abbey among the graves of his country's greatest men. He had grown to be a great pioneer, an explorer, a scientist, a doctor, a missionary, a freer of slaves.

In thirty years he travelled 29,000 miles, through the wild and unknown parts of Africa, exploring rivers, lakes, plains, forests, and mountains. He found out places where white settlers might make farms and plantations in health and safety. He sought for paths and waterways by which they might bring their cotton, grain, coffee, sugar, ivory, and skins to the seaports for sale. Among the black tribes he made many friends, doctored their sick, and lost no chance of showing them how to do their duty to God and make better use of their lives.

But his last and greatest work was to follow up the slave-hunters, and make known in England all the brutal and wicked horrors of the slave-trade. This was the work that wore him to death, but his noble self-sacrifice roused his countrymen to take possession of Central Africa and put an end to slavery. And if we look into his life, we shall find that the power to do all this came little by little, and day by day, from one simple source, namely, his earnest and unselfish desire to show his love for God by doing good to men. He was always trying to help and befriend others, and this made other men befriend him and give him the means of carrying on his work.

Livingstone's forefathers were Scotch Highlanders, and lived in the lonely island of Ulva, till hard times drove the family to settle in the village of Blantyre, among the Lanarkshire cotton-mills, where work was more plentiful.

Here David was born in the year 1813. His father, Neil Livingstone, an honest, steady, and hard-working man, took a great interest in all that was going on in the world. He was a great reader in many subjects, but was especially fond of books on missionary work. From him David inherited his Highland pluck and hardihood, and also his thirst for every kind of knowledge.

His mother, Agnes Hunter, came of an old family which, in the days of the Covenanter persecution, had been driven from home to the hills, and had risked torture and death rather than do what they believed to be wrong. She gave him her gentle and kindly nature, and taught him to be neat, orderly, and exact. From her tender but firm upbringing also, he gained the brave grip of truth, honour, and justice that makes men do and dare all things for duty's sake.

This was his heritage from his parents, and it proved of more value to him than all the money on earth.

At the village school of Blantyre David soon learnt to read and write. So poor, however, were his parents, that they had to take him away from his lessons at the early age of ten, and set him to work in a cotton-mill. Summer and winter, wet or fine, he had to appear at the factory at six in the morning, and stay there till eight at night, with short spaces allowed him for meals. Fourteen hours a day at the mill might well have broken his pluck and ruined his health, as, indeed, happened to many poor children, but David was made of harder stuff. He was bent on getting knowledge by some means or other. Very quickly he learnt to work the machine called the "spinning jenny," and was then raised to be a spinner with a small wage.

The first half-crown of his earning he took home, and slipped it into his mother's lap. To him it was a small fortune, and would have bought him many coveted things, but he thought of his mother's wants before his own. Later on, as he earned more wage, he bought himself books, and these he used to fix on the "jenny," snatching a few lines from them whenever he could spare an eye from his work. His hard and tiring day at the mill was long enough for any one, but in spite of this he joined night classes and sat up reading till sometimes his mother took away his books and drove him to bed.

His holidays were spent in ranging over the countryside with his brothers and sisters, and here too nothing escaped his keen eye and love of knowledge. Every animal, bird, insect, and plant was an interest to him, and he studied them closely, trying to find out all he could about their forms and habits. And while he thus began to learn the wonderful science of nature, he never dreamt that one day in the wilds of Africa he would use his knowledge in digging roots for his supper, or in avoiding vicious beasts and poisonous snakes.

As the years went on he grew restless, and was sometimes not very happy, without quite knowing why. In reality his mind was growing very fast, and wanted bigger and better work than watching the mill-wheels. Spinning cotton was useful enough in its way, but he wanted to do for mankind something greater and more lasting than that.

His father had many books and papers on mission work in China and India, and as David read of the wonderful beauty of these countries, and the ignorance and cruelty of their peoples, he sometimes thought he would like to be a missionary. The idea returned to him again and again, but he kept doubting whether he was the right person for the work. One day, however, when he was twenty years old, he happened to read a booklet that told such sad tales about the poor of China that his mind was troubled and stirred. So heavily did the story of human suffering and wrong weigh upon him that he began to take his country walks alone, in order to think the matter over undisturbed. Every morning he asked himself if he could do nothing to help, and every night he went to bed with the question still unanswered.

But at last there came an evening when he found an answer that made his way quite clear. He watched the sunset lights creep off the hills and clouds and die away in the growing starlight. He heard the thrush, all grateful for the joy of life, sing out its evensong till the calm hush of night stole over the tired world. The peace and beauty of it all seemed to make him sadder than ever. In such a lovely world, where there was room for all, food for all, and joy enough for all, it seemed to him so utterly strange that men could ever even want to cheat, rob, bully, and kill each other, and grab for themselves more than they could possibly use. The depth of his own sadness made him remember how once, in the stillness of the sunset hour, Jesus of Nazareth had wandered into an olive grove, and there had wept in bitter grief over the troubles of men.

Then suddenly the idea flashed into his mind that at least he could try and imitate the life of Christ as far as lay in his power. In a moment his mind was made up. He walked home with a brisk step and light heart, and told his parents that he was going to college at Glasgow to learn to be a doctor; and then he would go out to the far East to help the sick, and to tell men how they could make the world better and happier by imitating the life of Christ.

David lost no time in carrying out his plan, and at once began to put by all he could from his earnings at the cotton-mill. Want of money was his chief difficulty. Indeed, when at last he went up to Glasgow, he and his father walked all the way, and then had to trudge the streets till they found a lodging for David that cost no more than two shillings a week.

It was a hard struggle for young Livingstone, but still, by spending his savings very carefully, he managed to keep at his studies for a whole winter. Then he was forced to go back to the cotton-mills in order to save more money to pay for another winter's training. He was a quick and thorough learner, and at once it became quite clear to those who taught him that he would soon be fit for the life he had chosen.

Livingstone thought a good deal about the kind of a missionary he wanted to be. His idea of true mission work was to go among the people as a plain and simple man, trying every hour and minute of his daily life to do as Christ had done; and in this way he hoped to win their love and respect, and to lead them towards a nobler life of duty to God and man. At first he thought he did not need to study to be a preacher as missionaries usually did. But wiser friends showed him that if he became a missionary he would often have to preach to the natives, as well as live among them; and that he needed the regular course of study. So he offered himself to the London Missionary Society. The directors of the society examined him and sent him to Ongar in Essex for a three months' training among the other missionary students.

Here, with his usual care and thoroughness, he quickly learnt all that was set before him, but there was one thing he never could master: do what he would, he never could learn to preach. Once he was sent to a neighbouring parish with a most carefully prepared sermon; but he could get no further than the text, and so with a hasty apology he fled from the pulpit. Probably that was the only time in his life that he ran away from anything, but the event nearly ended his career.

His failure in preaching vexed the soul of his pastor so much, that Livingstone was sent back to the directors at the end of the three months with a bad report of his powers as a missionary. On the strength of this report he was nearly sent away as useless. One of the directors, however, who was wiser than his fellows, saw that Livingstone could both think well and do well, although he could not talk well. He accordingly took the young student's part, and insisted that he should have a further trial at Ongar. The result of this timely aid was that, after three more months of study, no one doubted Livingstone's fitness, and so in the year 1840 he was formally ordained a missionary.

Meanwhile, war had broken out in China, and no one could go there in safety. This was a disappointment to Livingstone, but while waiting for peace he would not be idle, so he went on with his medical studies at London, and also took his degree as a physician and surgeon at Glasgow. But the war still dragged on, and rather than waste any time, he decided to go to Africa; and accordingly, on 8th December 1840, he set sail for that vast and unknown continent, into which he was one day to bring new light, new hope, and new freedom.

FIRST YEARS IN AFRICA

THE sea voyage out to the Cape was a new life to Livingstone, and he made the most of it. With his usual determination to know all about everything, he made friends with the ship's captain, and soon began to learn how to manage the ship.

The captain taught him how to use a sextant and chronometer, two most important instruments, by whose help voyagers can tell exactly how far they are to the north or south, to the east or west. To "take an observation," as it is called, is no easy matter; but by hard and steady practice Livingstone in time became able to find out the ship's exact position and to mark it down neatly on the chart. And often in after life the captain's kindly teaching came to his aid when he lost his way in the wilds, or when he marked some new discovery on the map.

In his spare half-hours Livingstone would enjoy the many delights and wonders of the southern sea. He watched the dazzling little flying-fish dart like tiny rainbows from beneath the bows, glimmer over the water, and flash into the white comb of a wave. The dolphins, too, like clowns of the sea, amused him with their antics as they leapt and turned somersaults over the waves or sportively raced, two or three abreast, close ahead of the cut-water. Occasionally a monster sperm-whale would rise to the surface like a floating islet, spout his double fountain into the air, and plunge down again into his home. Sometimes, also, a grim and wicked-looking shark would prowl about the ship's wake in the greedy hope of human prey.

13

At last the long voyage was over and Livingstone landed at Cape Town. Here he found more sights and wonders awaiting him. He kept his eyes open, observing the customs of the natives, and especially the methods of missionary work. He soon found out that there were enough missionaries in this southern tip of the African continent to teach and preach to all the black men that lived there. He saw that new missionaries ought to go farther north where there were more natives and fewer mission stations.

Livingstone was very glad to do this himself. Although it would have been pleasanter and more comfortable to settle down where there were more white people, he was eager to do what was best for the black people he had come to help. In his student days he had decided to go to Africa because he had heard Dr. Moffat say, "I have sometimes seen in the morning sun, in the vast plain to the north, the smoke of a thousand villages where no missionary has ever been." David Livingstone decided then that he could make his life count for most in the regions of most need. And now that he had reached Africa, he saw that he was right.

So, during these first weeks in Africa, Livingstone made two plans: first, to make mission stations far up in the thickly-peopled native districts, and win over the most powerful chiefs; next, to make a training college whence native teachers could afterwards be sent to educate the many tribes. It was the first of these plans that decided the course of his after life, for he now was very sure that he could do better service to his cause by pioneering Central Africa than by settling down at the Cape to preach.

After a short stay at the Cape, Livingstone was sent into Bechuanaland to Kuruman, the most northern of all the mission settlements in South Africa. This station was worked by a good and capable missionary, Dr. Moffat, who was then away in England, and Livingstone had been ordered to await his return. Livingstone, however, did not mean to be idle, so he decided to spend the time in exploring the almost unknown country to the north of the station.

Accordingly he made a number of journeys in many directions, travelling about from tribe to tribe until he had thoroughly learnt the nature and resources of the country, and also the language and character of the natives.

On the first of these journeys Livingstone had an object-lesson in slavery that set his noble heart aching for the freedom of Africa. One day when he had outspanned his oxen for rest and food, he suddenly noticed that a young native girl had crept into camp, and was hiding under his waggon. He gave her some food, and in answer to his questions she told him her story. She and her sister had been left orphans, and they had lived happily together till the latter died. Then she was taken by another family, who kept her, not out of kindness, but with the cruel intention of selling her to some chief as a slave wife. On learning what was in store for her she ran away, meaning to trudge behind the waggon all the way to Kuruman, where she had friends.

While thus telling her tale, her face suddenly fell with fear, and she burst into tears. Livingstone looked up and saw that a native, armed with a rifle, had come to claim the poor child and take her back to slavery.

Livingstone could not bear the thought of giving her up, but he was at his wits' end to know the best way of saving her, till one of his native teachers, named Pomari, came to the rescue. The girl was attractive enough, with her bright eyes, white teeth, and soft, healthy skin, and her captors had loaded her in savage fashion with strings of beads. Pomari stripped the beads off the girl, and gave them to the man, who, after a little persuasion, took the bribe and went his way. Livingstone took care to keep the girl out of sight till they were safe out of the district. *12.10.2|*

Many other adventures befell the missionary on his travels; for wild animals, drought, fever, cattle-sickness, and the deadly tsetse-fly, whose bite kills oxen and horses in a few hours, always bring risk and excitement to an African journey. Once, when he was "trekking" several hundred miles through Bechuanaland in an ox-waggon, the fatal cattle-sickness fell like a plague upon his oxen and killed them all.

There was nothing to be done but to desert the waggon and tramp home. Livingstone's native servants were afraid that their master would never be able to do it. One of them pointed to his trousers and said, half in anxiety, half in scorn, that he was not really strong enough, and only put his legs into those bags to make them look stout. Livingstone, however, proved their fears groundless, and won their respect by walking them nearly to a standstill.

Once, too, he travelled 400 miles on ox-back, and found it awkward and uneasy work to keep his seat and avoid the sweep of the poor beast's horns as it shook off the flies that clustered round its eyes and nostrils. During this journey he fell down and broke his finger, and set the bone with his other hand. Not long after, a lion sprang out of the bush and raided their camp. Livingstone frightened the animal away by firing his revolver, but the kick of the weapon broke his finger anew.

Another time he had to fly for his life and hide from an angry rhinoceros which he had disturbed while she was feeding her calf. Upon missing him, the vicious brute charged full tilt at his waggon, and with the deadly upward stroke of her horn (a stroke which has been known to kill an elephant), splintered the wheel like match-wood.

All this while Livingstone was making friends of the tribes along his track. His manly fearlessness, his good humour and keen sympathy, his kindly eyes full of honesty and truth, soon showed the natives that there was nothing to fear from him. His medical skill got him the fame of a wizard, and black patients from far and near thronged his waggon to be cured of their ills, while some spread the report that he had brought dead men back to life.

Apart from this, he had a most wonderful gift of finding his way into the hearts of men; and though the natives could not understand the reason of his coming, yet they soon saw that he had not come, like some of the Transvaal Boers, to shoot them down, plunder their cattle, and carry off their children to a life of unpaid labour.

One chief, Bubé, was in difficulty for want of water for his crops. Every tribe had a sorcerer, who was supposed to have the power of bringing down rain when required; but Bubé's rainmaker had failed to supply him. Livingstone, however, taught them a surer way than sorcery, for he induced the whole tribe to turn out and dig a ditch from the river to their village, and by thus saving them from famine he won their love and respect. Bubé's faith in witchcraft afterwards cost him his life. His sorcerer vowed he could take the devil out of some gunpowder by the use of certain burning roots. Poor Bubé innocently went to watch the performance, and both were blown out of existence.

At last, after long waiting, Livingstone got leave from the directors to start a new mission-station, and this he did with the help of a brother missionary at Mabotsa, a place 250 miles north of Kuruman. Here Livingstone had to build a house for

THE STORY OF DAVID LIVINGSTONE

himself at his own expense, and as his income was only £100 a year, he built it with his own hands.

His work, however, was delayed by a misadventure that left him with a weak arm for all his days. A lion one day fell upon a flock of sheep near the village and began to kill them right and left. Livingstone went out for a little while to encourage the natives to surround it. The lion, however, broke away from its pursuers, and suddenly sprang out of the bush upon Livingstone: then, pinning him down with a paw on his head, it began to crunch the bone of his arm. A faithful follower, Mebalwé, diverted the beast from his master, and was himself attacked, but was saved by the lion falling dead of its wounds.

As soon as his arm was well enough, Livingstone finished his house, and then he brought home Mary Moffat from Kuruman to be his wife. They worked together to help the natives, and were successful and much loved. Mrs. Livingstone was very busy keeping house and teaching a big school of black children. Livingstone said that he was "Jack of all trades," and his wife "'maid of all work." While they lived here, a little son, Robert, was born, and after this the natives called Mrs. Livingstone Ma-Robert.

When a new missionary came to Mabotsa, Livingstone moved on to Chounane, 40 miles farther north, in the country of a chief called Sechélé. Water, however, was so scarce at Chonuane that Livingstone persuaded Sechélé's people to move with him still farther north, to Kolobeng. Here, for the third time, he built himself a house, but he did not dwell there for many years. His great mind ran continually upon the welfare of Africa, and he was always planning how best to uplift the millions who had not been reached by missions.

He now believed the best plan would be for Christian emigrants to come and teach the natives useful arts and industries, and to show them by example how to lead better lives.

But where was he to make his first little colony? East of Kolobeng lay the Transvaal, and the Boers, who hated him for his efforts against slavery, kept sending him threatening messages. North and west of him was the dry and trackless Kalahari Desert. He had heard native rumours about a large lake beyond the desert. There he might find a place suitable for his purpose; but he could not afford to pay for the waggons, cattle, native servants, and stores necessary for the journey across the desert. House-building had already cost him beyond his means. What was he to do?

The matter was settled for him by the generosity of an English gentleman, William Cotton Oswell, who had made several hunting trips in South Africa after big game, and had often been helped by Livingstone's knowledge of the country and language. Noble, fearless, and unselfish himself, Oswell had been from the first drawn into fast friendship with Livingstone; and now he offered to pay the cost of the expedition. Livingstone was overjoyed at his goodness, and on May 27, 1849, the expedition left Kolobeng. They had with them eighty oxen, twenty horses, and about twenty-five natives, and the fact that a waggon and span of oxen costs about £125 will give some idea of Oswell's generosity.

BEYOND THE KALAHARI DESERT

A GLANCE at the maps of Africa published before the year 1850 will show how little was known about the middle of the continent. All round the coast and a few hundred miles up the rivers there were plenty of names, but the centre was left almost blank. Most people supposed that the Great Sahara Desert in the north stretched down to the Kalahari Desert in the south. Cleverer men, however, thought of the enormous flow of water in the Nile, Congo, and Zambesi, and felt sure that somewhere there must be a land of streams, forests, and hills, vast enough to feed such mighty rivers.

In the exciting hope of pioneering this new land, and in the noble desire of bringing a better way of life to its peoples, Oswell and Livingstone dared the hardship and danger of the Kalahari. Oswell was to manage the trek, and the hard and tiring task of shooting enough game for the camp pot depended upon his quick eye, cool head, and steady hand. Livingstone was to be interpreter and scientific observer, while the party relied upon his wonderful power of gaining the goodwill of the natives.

They started from Kolobeng in a north-easterly direction, and for the first 120 miles their track lay through country they had passed before. Then they struck north towards the desert, and from this point they knew nothing of the country before them. One of the natives with them had crossed many years ago, and *thought* he could remember his route, but his memory proved very hazy.

With this man as guide, they came to the wells of Serotli, on the edge of the desert, and found that the place was just a dip in the sand, surrounded by low scrub and a few stunted trees. In the dip, however, were several little hollows, as though a rhinoceros had been rolling in the sand; and in one of these hollows lay about a quart of water.

Oswell at once set the party to work with spades and land turtle-shells to deepen the holes, but hard toil till nightfall only brought enough water to give the horses a mouthful or two each. Their guide told them that this was their last chance of water for 70 miles, so Oswell sent the oxen back to their last watering-place. Bellowing and moaning with disappointment and distress, the poor beasts crawled back 25 miles, and at last found relief from the terrible thirst they had suffered for ninety-six hours.

Meanwhile four of the Serotli pits were dug out to the depth of 8 feet, and water trickled into them so plentifully that Oswell sent for the oxen. On their arrival they were at once watered, inspanned, and headed across the desert. The heat was very great, and the wheels sank so deep into the loose sand that their utmost efforts only dragged the waggons 6 miles before sundown. On the following day they covered 19 miles without water. On the third day again these gallant beasts struggled 19 miles through the heavy sand in the smiting heat without a drop to drink.

That night was a bad one for the leaders of the expedition. They had now come 44 miles from Serotli at a rate of only 2 miles an hour, and the guide told them they were still 30 miles from the next water which was at a place called Mokokonyani the bushmen of the desert.

The oxen were spent with toil and thirst, and all night lay moaning out to their masters a piteous appeal for drink. No one knew for certain what lay before them, or whether they were in the right direction. Failure seemed more than likely, but Oswell and Livingstone were not the men to know despair. At the first sign of daybreak they sent the horses forward with the guide to try and find Mokokonyani. With the horses safe, the men could cover the ground in safety, and hunt for food on the way.

Oswell and Livingstone intended to follow with the waggons as long as the oxen could hold out; then they would loose the oxen on the trail of the horses in the hope that, without their burdens, they would mostly reach water alive. Half an hour after starting, the waggons passed through a belt of scrub, and came suddenly upon the horses at a dead halt. "Is it water?" was on every lip. No such luck was in store for them: the guide had lost his way.

Soon the weary oxen staggered in distress, and were outspanned to rest while the leaders took counsel for the future. Meanwhile the natives scattered through the scrub in a forlorn hope of finding water. Presently one of them heard the harsh croaking of a frog. No sweet music could fall softer on his ear, for where there is a frog there is always water close by. He ran back, and reported the discovery of a patch of marsh. Once more the jaded oxen were inspanned. The sense of water in the air seemed to revive them, and in two brisk miles they reached relief.

For the present, at all events, the expedition was saved. And it was well for them that they came upon the marsh, for it took them four more days to reach Mokokonyani, though on the first and third days they were luckily able to find water by digging. It turned out that they were in the bed of a "sand river" called the Mokokoong by the bushmen. Deep down below their feet a constant flow of water crept at a snail's pace through the sand. The course of the stream could be roughly traced like the long-dried bed of an ancient river. Sometimes it lay between ridges of naked limestone or banks of sand; sometimes it was lost in the level plain. In a very few places there were sand-holes deep enough to reach the stream, and here patches of marsh formed, or water showed in plenty, as at Mokokonyani. Otherwise there was no sign of water, though the bushmen get enough to quench their thirst by sucking through a long reed thrust down into the sand.

The party now tried to follow the sand river, but soon lost it for two waterless days. Then they found and followed it once more, until the underground stream disappeared in a marsh. At this point their guide again failed them, and they went many miles out of their course without water for three days. Here again fortune favoured them, for Oswell's eagle eye spied a bushwoman lurking in the thick scrub. He gave chase and captured her, and for a few beads she led them to a water-hole.

And now from a hillock they could see new and fertile country in the distance, with thick smoke rising beyond. It must be reeds burning on the shore of the great lake, they thought, and so pushed onward.

In a few more days they suddenly burst through the thick bush upon a wide and deep river, and from the natives on its banks they learnt that this was the Zouga, flowing from the great Lake Ngami, 250 miles up stream. It was now 4th July and late in the season, but for twelve more days they forced and jolted their waggons along the river bank until the oxen were nearly spent. Then Oswell and Livingstone picked out a span of the fittest, and pressed forward with a light waggon.

As they neared the lake the bush grew denser, and in the space of 5 miles they cut down more than one hundred small trees to let the waggon pass. At last, on 28th July, they reached Lake Ngami, having taken nine weeks to cover the 600 miles between them and Kolobeng.

Beyond the Zouga lay a fertile land of forest and plains, but the failure to reach it took away half the joy of their discovery. They could not get the waggons across, though Livingstone, at the risk of his life from alligators, spent many hours in the water vainly trying to make a raft. They were forced to return—Livingstone to Kolobeng, and Oswell to England; but they made plans to come again the next year, and Oswell promised to bring up a boat.

Next year, however, their plans failed, for Oswell was delayed, and Livingstone started without him. He took with him his wife and children, and, in spite of the hardships of the desert, they reached the Zouga and Lake Ngami in safety. Here fever fell upon the children, and he was forced to return. On the way back he met Oswell, who had followed only a few weeks' march behind.

Nothing could be done that year, but in 1851 these two great men again crossed the Kalahari Desert, taking with them Mrs. Livingstone and the children. This time Oswell, with his usual unselfish care for others, went a day in advance and dug out the wells, and thus the rest of the party were saved from delay and thirst.

They passed the Zouga in safety, and then, in a lovely land of fruits, flowers, and herds, they crossed stream after stream until they came to a point on the River Chobi 400 miles from Linyanté. Linyanté was the headquarters of the Makololo tribe, and their wise and powerful chief hurried to meet the travellers. He was quite overcome by his first sight of white men, but Livingstone's genial kindness soon set him at his ease, and then no one could have done more to help them. Sebituani told them all he knew about the country in and around his borders. Far to the north-west, he said, there lived a tribe who once sent back to him his present of an ox, and asked for a man to eat instead. From the east there came black messengers from the Portuguese with calico and beads and guns in exchange for slaves.

He promised to take his white friends ten days north of Linyanté to the mighty River Seshéké, which fell, men said, over a cliff into a chasm with a smoke and thunder that sounded many miles. Unfortunately this noble chief, whom Oswell decribed as a "gentleman in thought and manner," died of pneumonia a few days after; but his tribe kept all his promises to the explorers.

Leaving Mrs. Livingstone with the waggons in camp at the Chobi, the two friends went by canoe to Linyanté, and thence on horseback to the Sesháké. Here they indeed saw a mighty river, which proved to be the great Zambesi; but the waterfall was said to be far off, and the season was so late that once more they turned homewards.

On the way back many new plans were made. They had just been on the southern border of a country whence vile and brutal white men were getting slaves at the rate of eighteenpence apiece. If only they could find a good road into this country, honest trade might put an end to this wicked robbery of human lives. The road they had already found was too long and difficult, so Livingstone determined to revisit Linyanté the next year, and then seek a possible path to the sea-coast. It would be impossible for his family to go with him, and the thought of leaving them to the risks and dangers of Kolobeng was a great trouble to his mind.

Once more the goodness of his companion came to his aid. For Oswell persuaded Livingstone to send his wife and children to England, and also gave him the money for their outfit and expenses. He sold the ivory that had fallen to his rifle, and handed the price of it to his friend as a share of the game on their new preserves.

FROM COAST TO COAST

LIVINGSTONE took his family to Capetown, and saw them safely on board a ship bound for England. War was going on at the time with the Kaffirs, and he soon found that the white folk at the Cape looked on him with mistrust and dislike. They accused him and other missionaries of stirring up and helping the natives to rebel, and they even tried to prevent him from buying gunpowder for use on his journeys.

There were many, however, who believed in him, and amongst these was Maclear, the Astronomer-Royal. From him Livingstone had more lessons on "taking his bearings," and also learnt the use of an instrument for telling exactly how many feet any place stood above the level of the sea.

On his return northwards Livingstone was delayed by feeble oxen and a broken wheel, and thus he reached Kuruman only in time to learn that his home, the last he ever had, was in hopeless ruin.

Six hundred Boers under Pretorius came to Kolobeng, carried off everything of value in his house, and wrecked the rest. Even the leaves of his precious diaries and notebooks were torn and scattered to the winds. Moving onward to the native village, the Boers went morning and afternoon to the mission service and heard Mebalwé preach. After service they told Sechélé, the chief, that they had come to fight because he let Englishmen pass through his country. Surrounding the village, they fired the huts, and with long-range swivel-guns shot down sixty of the men, women, and children, who were huddled together on a hillock in the blinding smoke.

When the flames were spent the Boers closed in to finish their brutal work; but Sechélé held them at bay till nightfall, and sent them back to count their dead. Thirty-five Boers paid the price of this needless cruelty, while Sechélé and his remnant escaped under cover of the night.

To avoid the Boers, Livingstone passed well to the west of Kolobeng, and reached Linyanté after much hardship. The rainy season had flooded the land between the rivers, and his hands and knees were cut and torn from wading through reeds and pushing his way through the thorny bush. Sekelétu, the son of Sebituani, was now chief of the Makololo, and he soon grew fond enough of Livingstone to say "he had found a new father." With an escort and supplies from his "new son," the missionary made a tour through the Barotsi country, but could find no place fit for a settlement. The whole district was too unhealthy for white men, and the natives were unpromising.

Plunder and tyranny seemed the custom of the country. Here, for the first time in his life, Livingstone saw a string of slaves trudging along in hopeless misery beneath their chains. Once a mother was leading her little boy by the hand along the track, when suddenly a man pounced upon the child, and dragged him away shrieking to lifelong slavery.

Accordingly, in November 1853, Livingstone left Linyanté to carry out his plan of finding a way to the west coast. He set out with an escort of twenty-seven Makololo, and went by canoe up the Zambesi and Leeba, till some falls in the latter stopped him. From this point he went forward on ox-back, and, steering by compass as best he could, reached Loanda, in Portuguese country, in May 1854.

The troubles and difficulties of the journey were great. His medicine-chest was plundered, and his portable boat was lost. He was twice thrown from his ox, once on his head upon the hard ground, and once in the middle of a ford. He had thirty-one attacks of fever, and had to be his own doctor and nurse. His Makololo were cowards, and often wanted to go back, but Livingstone's patient courage turned them into men. Many of the tribes were very troublesome when he asked leave to pass their borders. One chief refused to let him go by unless he gave up a riding-ox, a gun, or a male slave; but Livingstone's wonderful force of character overcame his demand. At Chiboqué the natives refused to sell him food, and threatened to kill him if he did not give them an ox. They crowded round him, yelling and waving their spears and clubs over his head. Livingstone stood his ground with unflinching eye, and his fearless spirit utterly quelled them.

Another chief demanded his riding-ox or his life, and got the reply that he might kill him if he liked, but God would judge. The savage felt that he was in the presence of a greater chief than himself, and quailed before him. So great, indeed, was the power of Livingstone's presence that he once released a string of slaves by merely ordering their captors to let them go. A magic-lantern, with pictures from the Bible, helped him much in the management of the natives. They flocked to see it, though many were in terror lest the figures moving off the screen should enter into them as evil spirits. Livingstone humorously said that this was the only service they ever asked him to repeat.

When almost at his journey's end a party of natives stopped him at a ford on the Quango, in Portuguese country. Livingstone had little left to give away, so he handed over his razors and then his shirts, while the Makololo parted with their copper ornaments. This, however, was not enough; and Livingstone was just giving up his blanket and coat when a Portuguese sergeant came up and drove the natives away.

At last they reached Loanda, and the Makololo, who had never seen the ocean, were filled with delighted wonder. The houses in Loanda were strange and interesting to them, but most amazing of all was the British cruiser which lay in the harbour. The captain of this ship begged Livingstone to sail back with him to England. But Livingstone, though ill and weary and longing for his home and family, refused to go. He had promised to take the Makololo back to Linyanté, and he would not break his word to these black men who trusted him. So he sent off his letters and scientific notes in the *Forerunner*, and then started for Linyanté. The Portuguese had given his men bright-coloured suits, and had sent a uniform for Sekelétu. *16.09.22.*

They had not gone far when news came that all Livingstone's papers had been lost in the wreck of the *Forerunner*. He had to write the notes again, and this kept him from reaching Linyanté till September, 1855.

On their arrival, Sekelétu and his whole tribe turned out to meet them, and the party entered the town in triumphal procession, with the red and blue uniforms of the Makololo bearers in the van. Livingstone then held a service of thanksgiving, but the attention of his congregation was hopelessly upset by the glory of Sekelétu in the dress of a Portuguese colonel.

Livingstone did not remain long at Linyanté. The route to Loanda was too difficult and unhealthy for general trade, so he decided to follow the Zambesi down to the east coast, in the hope of finding a better. Sekelétu gave him a new escort of one hundred and twenty Makololo, and also supplied him with three riding-oxen, and ten more to be used for food.

In November 1855 he found the waterfall that Oswell and he had marked on their charts from hearsay, but had never seen. Here the great Zambesi, more than a mile wide, plunged "like a downward smoke" 300 sheer feet into a chasm, and then went seething and swirling away through a narrow zigzag rift. Twice as large as the Canadian Niagara, its spray darkened the sun above it, and its thunder boomed for miles. And, as in reverent silence he watched this mighty force flow on, Livingstone felt—

«These are Thy wondrous works, Parent of good,»

and he longed more than ever to see this lovely land in freedom and at peace.

Before leaving the "Mosi-oa-tunya," or the "Sounding Smoke," Livingstone changed its name to the Victoria Falls; but he little thought that in less than fifty years a railway bridge would span the gorge down which its waters swept.

Keeping mainly to the north bank of the Zambesi, he made his way to Teté, with much the same experience as usual. While his men and stores were crossing the Loangwé, he kept some unfriendly natives quiet by amusing them with his watch and burning-glass till all were safe. Once he was mistaken for a half-caste Portuguese slaver, and only saved his life by showing the colour of his breast and arms. His riding-ox took a determined dislike to his umbrella, and would not permit him to use it; so he suffered much from the rain, and even had to carry his watch in his arm-pit to keep it dry. At Teté he left his Makololo bearers, and, promising to return to them some day, made his way on to Quilimane.

In one respect his great journey was a failure: he had not found a really good route to the sea. Nevertheless he had found out two facts unknown to the world before. First, Central Africa was not a desert, but could produce metals, coffee, cotton, oil, sugar, corn, and many other things needed for the world's use. Second, the natives were capable of being taught by gentleness and justice to make good use of their lives.

These facts he wrote to the King of Portugal, telling him also that canals and roads could be easily made by the natives under good white leaders: then he set out for England to publish his knowledge in a book which he called "Missionary Travels."

He reached London in December 1856, and was at once lionised all over the kingdom. People were so full of encouragement that he felt it his duty to go on with the career he had begun. Even Queen Victoria, the Prince Consort, and Lord Palmerston sent for him to praise his work, while the Royal Geographical Society and other public bodies held meetings in his honour.

Livingstone was not at all spoiled by all this praise. He never liked much to talk about himself and the things he had accomplished, but he was glad that he could interest people in his beloved Africa.

He believed more and more that the best way to help the black millions of Africa was to open up their unknown country. This could only be done by exploring the rivers and making paths through the forests. Along these roads and waterways trade could be carried on and Christian people could travel over them, and so bring the light of civilisation into the heart of Central Africa.

So Livingstone was glad when the British Government offered to send him back to Africa as the leader of an expedition to explore the valley of the Zambesi. He was given the authority of Her Majesty's Consul, and a proper amount of money, supplies, and helpers.

THE ZAMBESI EXPEDITION

IN 1858 Livingstone once more set sail for the Cape, taking his wife with him, but leaving his children behind. At Cape Town the people were anxious to make amends for their former unkindness to him, and now did all they could to give him a happy welcome.

Continuing his voyage in the *Pearl*, up the east coast of Africa, he reached the mouth of the Zambesi, which enters the sea through many channels between low and swampy islands covered with thick jungle. The first thing to be done was to find out the deepest and safest of these channels, and many days were spent in sounding the depths of the water by sinking a lump of lead on the end of a line. An outlet called the Kongoné proved to be the best, and up this channel they took the *Pearl*.

Left and right the banks lay dark under the dense mangrove thicket, or shone bright with shrubs and flowers beneath tall palms and fern-trees, and forest timber laden and twined with creepers. Strange birds wheeled in bright flocks above them, or flashed in single brilliance across the stream. Here and there were open stretches where startled buffalo and zebra made off into the long grass, or a lazy rhinoceros could be heard wallowing and grunting out of sight among the giant reeds.

To those who had not seen this country before, it was indeed a new fairyland of wonders. The native huts were built high in the air upon long stakes, with ladders reaching from their doorways to the ground. Down these the natives came scrambling in eager haste to see the *Pearl*. Some of them took her for a floating village, and others asked if she was hollowed out of a single tree-trunk like their own canoes.

When the river became too shallow for so large a ship, Livingstone landed his stores on an island, and then went forward in a small steamer sent out by the Government for use on the Zambesi. The steamer proved to be a failure. She had been built to burn wood instead of coal; but it took all her crew three days to cut enough fuel to drive her for two days. She was so slow that native canoes easily outstripped her; and she snorted, and creaked, and wheezed to such an extent that she was nicknamed the *Asthmatic*.

This was a most grievous drawback to the expedition, but Livingstone, as usual, made the best of it. He took his stores to Shupanga, a Portuguese village near the point where the Zambesi is joined by another fine river called the Shiré. Then by slow degrees he made his way up stream to Teté, where he had left his Makololo bearers on his former visit. They were overjoyed to see him again: some of them rushed to embrace him, but others cried out, "Don't touch him, you'll spoil his new clothes." People had told them that Livingstone would never return, but the Makololo knew he would never break his word. "We trusted you," they told him, "and now we shall sleep."

Twenty miles above Teté the river broke through a chain of hills, and at this point the *Asthmatic* was stopped by the Kebrabasa Rapids. The river ran swiftly down a narrow valley, with the current broken here and there by jagged rocks or smooth water-worn boulders. At this season the river was at its lowest, and Livingstone decided to explore the rapids on foot; for he thought it might yet be possible for small steamers to pass them when the river was full.

Accordingly, he and his fellow-explorer, Dr. Kirk, set out with a native guide and some of the Makololo to make the matter sure. They followed up the bed of the river as best they could, taking measurements and notes as they went. Sometimes their way was over smooth terraces of rock, sometimes they scrambled over boulders, and once they had to wade up to their waists in spite of the risk of crocodiles. At night they slept under trees, and were lucky enough to be left alone by wild beasts, though a native across the river was killed one evening by a leopard.

When at last they reached the head of the rapids, their guide declared that now there was nothing but smooth water before them. Thinking their difficult task was at an end, they began to return, but that night two natives came into camp, and said there was another rapid a few miles up stream.

Taking three of the Makololo with them, Livingstone and Kirk went back again to settle the question. They found a narrow gorge, whose sides rose steeper than a gable roof from the river to the skyline, 2000 feet above them. Up this they scrambled, cutting their way through the prickly scrub, and crawling over the face of the sloping cliff. The sun struck into the gorge with such force, that the rocks reeked like heated steel; and the climbers' hands could hardly bear their grip long enough to gain firm foothold. Even the Makololo, whose naked soles were hard and tough as shoe-leather, limped with the pain of their burnt and blistered feet. They turned to Kirk, and said that Livingstone no longer had a heart, and must be stark mad to try and climb where no wild animal would go. Losing all heart, they wanted to lie down and sleep in the hollows, but Livingstone's pluck and spirit carried them through.

At last, after a scramble so steep and dangerous that they took three hours to climb one mile, the party reached a spot overhanging the rapid. Here the cliff dropped a hundred feet sheer into the stream, and rose like a wall just a short stone's-throw across it. Into this narrow pass the whole wide river was crowded, and the current sped swiftly down, broken here and there into a white fleece by a ridge of jutting rock. They saw the flood-mark, eighty feet up the opposite cliff. But Livingstone turned away in keen disappointment; for though a powerful steamer might stem the rapid at high flood, the river was use-less as a waterway for most of the year.

In 1859 Livingstone turned his attention to a branch of the Zambesi, called the Shiré. This river came slowly winding down a broad and fertile valley of forest and of plains, which stretched on either hand towards wooded hills with bare mountain-peaks beyond. Its banks were thick with leaf and blossom, and the air was filled with the scent of flowers, the song of birds, and the endless murmur of bees. Yet, as they passed up stream in the midst of all this beauty, the explorers could see the savage Manganja natives lurking behind trees, with bent bows, ready to shoot them down with barbed and poisoned arrows. Nothing happened, however, till the steamer came opposite the village of a chief named Tingané, who was a terror to the Portuguese, and had never yet allowed any man to pass his borders.

Here a crowd of five hundred Manganja lined the bank and ordered them to stop. Some of the savages even began to take aim with their fatal arrows, and it looked as though a ter-rible death would fall upon the explorers whether they obeyed or not. Livingstone at once went fearlessly on shore. He knew that he came for love of God, and he believed that he would not die till God no longer needed him to work on earth.

Calm and smiling, as if in a playground full of children, he walked through the bloodthirsty mob to their chief, and told him that the steamer was English and not Portuguese. Then he explained that the English wished to put down the cruel slave trade, and make it easier for black men to sell their cotton and ivory for cloth and beads.

Tingané liked the idea of this, and wished to hear more. Livingstone told him how the white man's book said that all men and women were sons and daughters of God, and therefore must not be treated with cruelty and unkindness. Thus Tingané was completely won over to friendship. He called his people together, and told them that the great white chief and healer of men had come with a good message, and might pass his borders in peace.

After this there was no more trouble with the Manganja, and the leaky *Asthmatic* puffed and panted safely up the river, scaring out of their wits the wild animals upon its banks. Now and then a clumsy hippopotamus, startled out of its sleep, would splash out of the water and tear into the jungle. Antelopes and zebras fled over the plains, and once the explorers disturbed a herd of more than eight hundred elephants. Wicked-looking crocodiles would sometimes dash for the steamer with open jaws; but, on finding that it was not good to eat, they would dive to the bottom like stones. The river was deep and free from sandbanks for 200 miles, but here the steamer was once more stopped by a chain of rapids stretching over 40 miles. These Livingstone named the Murchison Cataracts, and from this point he made two journeys on foot.

On the first trip he climbed over the mountains to the eastward, and found Lake Shirwa, whose waters were stagnant and bitter. His native guide told him there was a much larger lake to the northward; so Livingstone, after returning for supplies, once more started from the Murchison Cataracts in search of it.

The way led over the highlands of the Manganja country towards the head of the Shiré valley. The natives were warlike, but Livingstone had no trouble with them, and easily bought all the food he wanted with a few yards of calico or a handful of beads. The women wore their hair quite short, and disfigured themselves with a large ring of ivory or tin through the upper lip. The men kept their hair long, and did it in as many fashions as white women. Sometimes they stiffened it with strips of bark into the likeness of a buffalo's horn or tail; sometimes they shaved off patches in the shape of some wild animal, and then thought themselves very beautiful.

At last, on September 16, 1859, Livingstone came upon the magnificent Lake Nyassa, stretching away to the skyline like an inland sea. Out of its waters the River Shiré ran smooth and deep all down the long valley to the Murchison Cataracts. Forty miles of road could easily be made past these falls, and then the great Nyassa would be open to the sea. The uplands of the Shiré valley were healthy and fertile, and here at last was the place where a colony of Christian emigrants might teach and show the Africans a life of righteousness and industry. Moreover, Livingstone saw that, as all the slave traffic had to cross the river or the lake, a single small steamer could soon put an end to the trade.

He therefore wrote home, and promised £2000 from the price of his book to be spent in sending out suitable emigrants. At the same time he asked the Government for a new vessel to replace the dying *Asthmatic*, and he also offered £4000 towards a little steamer for Lake Nyassa. In the meantime, while waiting their arrival, he kept his promise to the Makololo, and started up the Zambesi to take them home to Linyanté.

THE UPPER SHIRÉ AND LAKE NYASSA

ON his return from Linyanté to Teté, Livingstone once more went on board the *Asthmatic*, and started to meet his new steamer at the mouth of the Zambesi. Some of the Makololo had refused to go back to their native country, and Livingstone was thus able to have a few of these faithful men with him still.

The poor *Asthmatic*, however, did not reach her journey's end. Her steel plates were rotten with rust, and she leaked in all directions. Her cabin floor was flooded, her bridge was broken down, and her engines groaned aloud. In this water-logged and rickety state she touched a sandbank, turned on her side, and sank, after giving her crew just enough time to save themselves and their stores in canoes.

A few weeks later, in June 1861, the new steamer, called the *Pioneer*, reached the mouth of the Zambesi. At the same time, there came a party of missionaries under the brave Bishop Mackenzie, who had been sent out by the Universities of Oxford and Cambridge to settle in the Shiré valley. Livingstone would have taken the mission party up the Shiré at once, but he was ordered by the Government to look for another way to Lake Nyassa, along the River Rovuma.

Taking the Bishop with him, he started immediately to carry out his orders, but the new steamer upset all his plans.

The *Pioneer* was a splendid little vessel, but she lay two feet deeper in the water than she ought, and so kept running aground on the sandbanks. After struggling a short distance up the Rovuma, Livingstone gave up the attempt, and returned with the *Pioneer* to take the mission party up the Shiré. Landing at the Murchison Cataracts, they made their way towards the Manganja highlands on foot.

The party had not gone very far before they learnt from the natives that gangs of slavers had been seen passing through the country with their captives. This was distressing news, and Livingstone now found out how false some of his Portuguese friends had been. The Portuguese had helped and encouraged Livingstone to make friends of the natives; then, as soon as he had gone, they had sent their servants on his tracks to make slaves. These brutal ruffians said they were "Livingstone's children," and so the natives let them pass into the heart of the country in peace. Then the slavers bribed a strong tribe to attack a weak tribe, and after the fight they made slaves of the captives. Livingstone's unexpected return caught some of these villains in the very act.

He had halted his party in a village for rest and food, when suddenly a long file of eighty-four slaves came round the hillside towards them. The captives, mostly women and children, were roped together with thongs of raw hide, but some of the men had their necks fixed in a "goree," or forked slave-stick. The back of the neck was thrust into the fork, and the two prongs were joined by a bar of iron under the chin, while a slaver walked behind, holding the shaft of the stick, ready to wring the poor slave's neck at the first sign of escape. Worn out with pain, misery, and fatigue, the hapless slaves limped and staggered beneath their loads. The slavers, decked out with red caps and gaudy finery, marched jauntily along, blowing tin horns and shouting as though they had just won a noble victory.

At the first sight of the little English party, these braggarts fled headlong into the bush; but one of the Makololo was too quick for their leader, and caught him by the wrist. Dragging him by the arm, and driving him with the terror of a spear-point, the Makololo brought the chief of the slave gang to Livingstone, who at once recognised him as a servant of the Portuguese chief officer at Teté.

The inhuman wretch said he had bought the slaves, but his prisoners told a different tale. They had been captured in war by the slavers, who had burnt their village, murdered their tribesmen, and marched them off in bonds towards Teté. On the way two of the women had tried to loosen the thongs that cut their flesh, and were instantly shot by their captors. One of the men sank down with fatigue, and was killed with an axe as a warning to the others. Another woman became too exhausted to carry her load as well as her baby. The heartless slavers tore the child from her arms and killed it with terrible cruelty.

Livingstone and his friends quickly set themselves to the work of cutting the thongs and sawing the slave-sticks off the captives, and while they were thus busy, the chief of the slavers escaped.

Continuing the journey, the Englishmen set free several parties of slaves in the next few days before reaching the village of Magomero. Here Chigunda, the chief, invited Bishop Mackenzie to settle; and, as the spot seemed a good one, Magomero was thus made the station for the Universities' Mission. All the freed slaves were joined to the mission, and the work of building was going on quickly, when word came that a tribe from the neighbouring Ajawa country were raiding slaves from a village close by. Livingstone and the Bishop thought that a friendly talk might win the Ajawa over to better ways, and a small party at once left the mission station to make the attempt. It was not long before they saw the smoke of a burning village, and then, hurrying forward over a hillside, they came upon the raiders making off with plunder and captives.

The Ajawa leader sprang on an anthill to count the missionary band, and Livingstone at once shouted that he had come in peace for a friendly talk. Unluckily, some Manganja followers called out the name of their great warrior, Chibisa, foolishly hoping to frighten the raiders away.

At once the Ajawa leaders raised the cry of "Nkondo! Nkondo!—War! War!" and all the raiders dashed to the attack. Keeping at a distance of about a hundred yards, they began to surround the little band. Some of the Ajawa danced like madmen, with hideous grimaces meant to strike terror into the white men's hearts. Others played clownish antics with their weapons to show how they would treat their foes. Others shot poisoned arrows from shelter behind trunks and stones, and wounded one man in the arm.

Still Livingstone tried bravely and nobly for peace, but in vain: the savages were like wild beasts thirsting for prey. Then some more of the raiders came up and began to fire with muskets. Livingstone was unarmed, but some of the party had rifles, and fired a few shots in reply. As soon as the Ajawa heard the sing of the rifle-bullets, they fled in a panic. Some of them shouted back that they would track the white men down, and kill them where they slept, but they never dared to return.

This was the first time that Livingstone had failed to make peace, and it was through no fault of his own. But for the foolish cry of the Manganja, he would most probably have succeeded.

He stayed at Magomero till he was obliged to return to the *Pioneer;* and his parting advice to the Bishop was never to interfere with the quarrels of the natives, and also to keep on the highlands, so as to escape the fever near the river.

Livingstone and Kirk now started to explore Lake Nyassa. A four-oared boat, fitted with a sail, was slung on poles, and carried to the head of the Murchison Cataracts by native bearers. Here they launched her, and with oar and sail passed along the smooth waters of the Upper Shiré, till they reached the lake. Keeping to the eastern coast, they passed bay after bay on a beautiful and fertile shore, backed by a grand range of purple hills. Cotton and corn grew well, and the explorers often saw men spinning, weaving, and sewing in the huts, while the women hoed the corn. The natives were great fishermen, and caught all kinds of fish with fine woven nets and ivory hooks of their own making.

The lake was subject to heavy storms, and once the explorers were caught a mile from shore by a furious squall. They could not land, for in a few minutes the billows ran so high, and broke upon the beach with such force, their little boat would have been dashed to splinters on the stones. All they could do was to hold her bows to the wind with their oars and try to outride the fury of the storm. Up on the crest, down in the trough, they fought it wave by wave for many hours, while every moment a chance of death went speeding by. As the white lip of each roller curled over, they held their breath, in doubt lest the threatening mass should break over the little boat and swamp her. Yet breaker after breaker went hissing and gurgling past on either hand, but not a single one struck her. At last, when the storm sank down, they were able to land with stiff and aching muscles, but with thankful minds.

After following the shore for nearly two hundred miles, the explorers were almost at the head of the lake when they had to turn back. Livingstone had arranged to go down the Zambesi to meet a ship from England which was bringing his wife to join his labours once more, and on board the same vessel were supplies for the *Pioneer*, and also the little steamer he had bought for use in putting down the slave trade on Lake Nyassa.

On their way down the Shiré, the *Pioneer* struck on a shoal, and there she had to stay for five weeks, till the river rose enough to float her again. At length Livingstone reached the sea, and found his wife on board the cruiser *Gorgon*, but the joy of their meeting was not to last long. A few weeks after her arrival, she was seized by fever at Shupanga. Day and night Livingstone nursed and tended her with his utmost skill and care, but all in vain. In April 1862 she died, and this was a sorrow that lasted all his days.

FOILED BY THE SLAVERS

LIVINGSTONE now made a second attempt to reach Lake Nyassa by the River Rovuma. The explorers started in rowing-boats with a party from the cruiser *Gorgon*, and made their way up stream for many days without much adventure, though twice their right of way was disputed.

Once a tribe of natives crowded both banks, and, while fitting poisoned arrows to their bows, began the hideous antics of their war dance. Their chief hailed the boats, and ordered the explorers to stop and pay toll. After a parley, Livingstone gave him thirty yards of calico, and he promised in return that his tribe would be their friends. No sooner, however, had the first boat rounded the next bend of the river, than a cloud of poisoned arrows and a few musket-balls came whizzing and singing over the heads of her crew. The sail was cut and torn, but luckily no one was wounded, and a few rifle-shots from the second boat sent the natives flying through the bush.

Another time a surly hippopotamus tried to stop their way. He seemed to think they had no right to cross his favourite bathing-pool, and wake him out of his mid-day sleep. Diving under the water, he came up just under the boat, and rocked her to and fro as he tried to lay hold of her with his clumsy jaws. After grinding away at her planks for a while with his teeth, he at last made up his mind that she was too big and too tough for him to swallow, and then he plunged off in a fit of the sulks.

When Livingstone had taken the boats as far up the Ro-vuma as possible, he found that the river was divided into two branches, and the natives told him that neither of them came from the Lake Nyassa. Accordingly he returned to Shupanga, and then for the last time started up the Shiré in the *Pioneer* with his own little steamer, the *Lady Nyassa*, in tow.

It was not long before he began to see that, even in the short time he had been away, the deadly slave trade had come like a blight on the land. A half-bred Portuguese, named Mariano, and his brutal gang had deceived Tingané by call-ing themselves "Livingstone's children," and so were treated as friends. Thus, taking him by treachery, they killed him and many of his tribe, and dragged off all they could to slavery. Not content with this, they burnt the village and the stores of corn, destroyed the crops, and drove away the flocks. No more corn would grow for many months, and those who escaped were thus left to starve. Many of them clung to life by hunt-ing game and digging up roots, but far the greater number of them died of famine.

When once Tingané was overcome, the work of the slavers was easier; for his tribe was the strongest, and had been the frontier guard. Village by village this foul and ruthless piracy spread up the river, till now Livingstone saw the whole face of the country changed.

The smiling valley he had found four years ago was now a land of death, strewn with black ruins and whitened skeletons. Even the song-birds were silent around the wasted homes, as though they could not bear to sing in the midst of such mis-ery and desolation. Yet the inhuman Portuguese were paying Mariano for his slaves, and Livingstone had not the power to stop them. All he could do was to push on with his work, and publish all he saw, in the hope that the British Government would interfere.

But fortune was against him completely. On reaching the Murchison Cataracts the explorers unscrewed the Lady Nyassa to pieces, and then began to make a road over which they could take her, bit by bit, to the head of the rapids. Before the first mile of this road was finished, both Kirk and Livingstone fell dangerously ill, and Kirk had to return to England.

At the same time a despatch came from the British Government to recall the expedition. The Portuguese Government had forbidden all ships but their own to enter the Zambesi, and the British did not think it worth while to interfere. A bitter disappointment like this might well have broken his spirit, but Livingstone was too brave and too faithful to his cause for that. The *Pioneer* must wait several months for the floods before she could go down the river, and meanwhile he would row round Nyassa in search of a way to the sea outside Portuguese country.

Once more his bearers started to carry a boat past the cataracts, and all went well till they came to a stretch of smooth but swift water below the uppermost rapid. Here, to save labour, the boat was launched and towed up stream with a rope from the bank. All their stores were put inside her, and also some of the Makololo, who kept her off the rocks with poles. After two miles the Makololo, who were splendid canoe-men, said the current was too swift and dangerous, and they brought the boat to the bank.

Then some conceited Zambesi canoe-men took hold of the poles and tow-rope, saying they would teach the Makololo how to take her up the rapid. Livingstone had moved on, away from the bank, and knew nothing of their intention till he heard loud shouts of distress. He rushed to the bank just in time to see his stores and the Zambesi men in the water, and his boat shooting keel uppermost down the river like a dart.

Some of the party gave chase, but the bank was too difficult for speed, and they never saw the boat again. The Zambesi men swam to shore and knelt down, with their foreheads touching the earth, at Livingstone's feet. He sent them down to the *Pioneer* for more stores, and, nothing daunted by this new disappointment, started off to go round Nyassa on foot. But in spite of all his efforts he did not reach the end of the lake before it was time to return to the *Pioneer* and make his last voyage down the Shiré.

The Universities' Mission also had come to an end for a while. The brave Bishop Mackenzie had lost his life from fever on a journey down the Shiré. The rest of the missionaries thought it best to move down from the highlands to the river bank, and one by one they died of fever. Livingstone now took the remnant of the mission away with him on board the *Pioneer*, lest they should again fall into the hands of the slavers.

In February 1864 he handed the *Pioneer* over to H.M.S. *Orestes*, at the mouth of the Zambesi, while his own little steamer was taken in tow to Zanzibar by the cruiser *Ariel*. Here he learnt that many people in England and at the Cape were blaming him for the failure of the Zambesi expedition, and also for the fate of the Universities' Mission. Livingstone felt this very keenly, for he knew that the chief blame lay with the slave trade. If the British Government had forced the Portuguese to put an end to slavery, there would have been no failure at all.

Defeated and disappointed as he was, Livingstone would not give in, for he knew that he was working in God's cause. He also firmly believed that, if he could only make his countrymen really understand the wicked cruelty and waste in

Africa, they would come to the rescue. Clearly it was his duty to awaken their understanding and show them the way when they came. He determined to visit England, and publish all he knew about Africa and the slave trade; then he would return to his pioneering, and find out more.

To get money for the voyage he now tried to sell the *Lady Nyassa*, but, on hearing that the Portuguese wanted her for a slave-boat, he decided to take her to Bombay.

This was one of the boldest feats he ever carried out. Taking with him a crew of three white men and nine natives, he started in the tiny little steamer to cross 2500 miles of the Indian Ocean with fourteen tons of coal. Two of his white sailors fell ill, and so for many days he and the third man shared the watch in spells of four hours. Then they lost the wind, and lay becalmed for twenty-five days, not daring to waste their coal. At last a breeze sprang up, and they were able to use their sails again; but they had to pass through two furious storms before their journey's end.

The good little *Lady Nyassa*, however, came safely through everything, till strands of seaweed and green and yellow sea-serpents told them they were near the coast of India. They had then only enough coal to last twenty-eight hours, and their supplies were nearly done; but still they managed to hold out and reach Bombay after a voyage of forty-five days. The *Lady Nyassa* was so small that no one noticed her arrival till Livingstone went on shore and made himself known.

In due time Livingstone reached England, and wrote an account of the expedition in a book called "The Zambesi and its Tributaries." He was sought out everywhere for speeches, lectures, and entertainments; but as soon as his work in England was finished he returned to Zanzibar to carry out the purpose of his life.

Before leaving England the Prime Minister sent to ask him if there was anything he wanted. Many men would have asked for money or a title, but Livingstone thought of nothing but his work. His only request was that the Government would make a treaty with Portugal to put down slavery and open the Zambesi to honest trade. He was then called before a committee of the House of Commons, who heard all his opinions about Africa and the slave trade. Yet all the Government did at the time was to give him £500 towards his expenses, and to make him Consul of Central Africa, but without a salary and without a pension. His friends in the Royal Geographical Society gave £1500 towards the new expedition, and Livingstone promised them to try and discover the true sources of the Congo and the Nile.

IN THE HEART OF AFRICA

IN March 1866 Livingstone landed near the mouth of the Rovuma, and, at the age of fifty-three, began the seven long years of hardship, misery, and pain that wore him to his death. Thirty-six bearers came with him, of whom thirteen were Sepoys from Bombay, and ten were natives of Johanna. Livingstone was very anxious to find some beast of burden which could stand the poison of the tsetse-fly; and for this experiment he brought with him some camels, Indian buffaloes, mules, donkeys, and a calf. Carrying stores was the great difficulty in his travels, and a few hardy beasts of burden, instead of a number of unruly knaves, would have saved him from the terrible want he afterwards had to suffer.

It was not long before his troubles began. The Sepoys had charge of the animals, and neglected them so shamefully that one by one the poor creatures died. Livingstone found he could not trust one of the thirteen out of his sight, and at last they grew so troublesome that he sent them back to the sea. His next discovery was that the ten natives from Johanna were rascals and thieves; and one of them, Musa, who had worked in the *Lady Nyassa*, turned out the worst of the lot. Moreover, the country had been ravaged by slavers, and food grew scarcer and scarcer, till at length they lived mainly on maize and the few pigeons and guinea-fowl shot by the way.

The signs of the slave trade were terrible. Here, as in the valley of the Shiré, nothing seemed too brutal to be done. Even women were tied to trees and left to starve, because they were too worn out to trudge any longer.

Most of the slavers in this district were Arabs, and they did all they could to make trouble for Livingstone. He reached Nyassa in August, at a point half-way up its eastern shore, and here he wanted to cross; but all the boats were in the hands of the slavers, and Livingstone could get nothing to take him over.

Determined not to be beaten, he walked round the south end of the lake, and, on crossing the Shiré, he came upon ground that he had passed before. Old times and old friends came into his mind, and he wondered sadly if all their labour had been wasted. He thought also of his faithful Makololo, and longed to have them in the place of his present bearers.

After passing round the south end of Lake Nyassa, he took a north-westerly direction, and came to the village of a chief named Marenga. Here they met an Arab slaver, who cunningly invented a story in the hope of frightening Livingstone's bearers from going any farther. He told Musa that a savage Mazitu chief was in front of them, killing all who passed his borders, with great cruelty. Musa believed this story, and refused to go onward. Livingstone tried to convince the coward that there were no Mazitu in the district, but all his efforts were useless. Musa and the other nine Johanna natives deserted in a body; but the rest of the bearers, much to the Arab's disappointment, remained faithful.

From Marenga's Livingstone pushed on towards Lake Tanganyika, and his hardships daily grew greater. Owing to the slave trade, food was scarce, and the natives had little to sell. For many days the explorer lived on African maize, helped down with milk from some goats he had brought for the purpose. The next misfortune was the loss of his goats, and this left him to break and loosen his teeth on the tough, hard maize, while he dreamed of delicious and savoury dinners.

This want of food made him very weak, and, moreover, the toils of the march were great. Often he had to wade through marshes up to the waist; and after the burning day, with its clouds of flies, there came the damp heat of night, with clouds of mosquitoes bringing fever in their poisonous bite. All this was trouble enough, but worse still happened.

One day a native bearer, possibly bribed by a slaver, disappeared with Livingstone's medicine-chest, and he was now left defenceless against fever. Soon he became so ill that he sometimes lay insensible on the ground; but still his pluck carried him through, and at last, in April 1867, he reached Chitembé's village, on Lake Tanganyika, where he found rest and better food.

Meanwhile, Musa and the other Johanna natives had gone back to Zanzibar. They knew they would get no pay if their bad conduct was found out, so they swore that Livingstone was dead, and therefore they were obliged to return. Musa made up a clever story describing how Livingstone had been attacked by natives, and had died fighting bravely, while the faithful Johanna men, after escaping from the fight, had returned at nightfall to bury their beloved master. Musa repeated this lie so skilfully that every one believed him; and even Dr. Kirk, who was now at Zanzibar, was taken in completely. The tale was told at home in the papers, and all his countrymen were grieving for his loss, when an Englishman, Edward Young, began to doubt the story. Young had been on the *Lady Nyassa* with Musa, and knew that the rascal's word could never be trusted. He laughed at the idea of a coward like Musa returning after a fight to bury any one, and he found other faults in his story.

At last the Royal Geographical Society sent Young to Africa to find out the truth. He went up the Shiré in a steel boat called the *Search*, and his bearers carried her in pieces past the Murchison Cataracts. Then, launching her again on the Upper Shiré, he made his way by Lake Nyassa to Marenga's country. Here he found out the utter falsehood of Musa's story, and learnt that Livingstone had been seen alive on his way to Tanganyika.

Young now returned to England; and, though his news was mainly good, yet many people were still very anxious about the explorer's safety. In one way Musa had done his master a good turn without the least intention. For so much had been said in the papers about Livingstone, that people began to see how great was his work and how noble his life.

All this time Livingstone knew nothing either of Musa's lies or of Young's gallant search. While at Chitembé's village he heard of a chain of lakes joined by a big river, and he started westward to find them. Slave-raiding was going on all over the country that lay before him; but in spite of this Livingstone discovered Lake Moero, in November 1867, after suffering terribly from illness and want of food. A beautiful river, called the Luapula, ran into the lake at the south, and out again to the north. Down stream, to the northward, the natives said the Luapula reached a long lake of many islands; while up stream, to the southward, they said it came from a large lake, called Bangweolo.

Livingstone decided to look for Bangweolo first. Setting out from Moero in a southerly course, he came to the village of Kazembé, a chief who punished his people by cutting off their hands and ears. At Kazembé's he fell in with an Arab trader, Mohammed Bogharib, who at once took a great liking to the explorer. Mohammed asked him to dine, and Livingstone sat down on a mat to a feast of vermicelli and oil, meal cakes and honey; and then, the first time for many months, he warmed his heart with a bowl of good coffee and sugar.

From the accounts of the natives, Bangweolo was only ten days' march from Kazembé's, but now Livingstone's bearers refused to go onward. Five only remained faithful to the kindest master they ever had, and with these the journey was begun. It was the same tale of hardship and toil, want and suffering; and, since the theft of his medicine-chest, there was nothing to soothe the fever or ease the pain. Yet through all this his patient faith and quiet valour carried him on, and, in July 1868, he came upon the beautiful Lake Bangweolo. There were islands dotted about in it, and Livingstone visited some of them in a native canoe; but, when he wanted to paddle across the lake, his canoe-men refused. They were afraid of being made slaves.

Indeed, the curse of slavery seemed everywhere in the land. On his way to Bangweolo, Livingstone had passed some slaves trudging along in their slave-sticks, yet singing as they went. Their only hope was death; and they were looking forward with revengeful joy, because they ignorantly believed their spirits could return and kill their captors. The meaning of their chant was, "Oh, you send me to the sea-coast, but my yoke is off in death; back I'll come to haunt and kill you." Then, as a chorus, they hissed between their teeth in bitter hatred the names of those who had robbed them of their freedom.

Livingstone now struggled back to Kazembé's, utterly worn out with toil, hunger, and fever. Here he found Mohammed Bogharib on the point of returning to Ujiji, and he gladly accepted the Arab's kind offer of an escort thither. Ujiji stood upon the eastern shore of Tanganyika, and also was on the main slave-route to Zanzibar. Before leaving Zanzibar, in the

February of 1866, Livingstone had arranged with Dr. Kirk to send stores, medicine, letters, and newspapers to await him at Ujiji, and now he looked forward to news of his children, and relief from sickness and pain.

The journey was a terrible one; for Livingstone grew worse and worse, till at last he grew dazed with fever and pain, and lost count of the days. Mohammed saved his life by having him carried in a hammock till they reached the west shore of Tanganyika, and took canoe to Ujiji. The voyage of eighteen days, and the hope of his letters and medicine, revived him greatly, and he landed at Ujiji with joy. But the two men in charge of his stores had sold nearly all of them for ivory and slaves, and his medicines and mails had been left at Unyany-embé, thirteen days distant, while the road there was blocked by a slave war.

It was now March 1869, and he had not seen a white man's face, or heard of his children, for three years.

A DEATHBLOW TO SLAVERY

LIVINGSTONE at once wrote to Kirk at Zanzibar for more stores to be sent to Ujiji. At the same time he sent a letter to the Sultan of Zanzibar, asking him for fifteen trustworthy bearers to carry the new supplies. Then, as soon as could be, he collected the remnant of his plundered things, and wrote his letters and accounts of his doings. One or two letters reached him here, but these were nearly three years old; and very many of his own to his friends never got even as far as the sea-coast. At a single time he sent off a budget of forty-two letters and scientific records, but none were heard of again.

The reason of this was only too plain. Ujiji was like a den of villains and thieves. All the worst of the slave-trading Arabs gathered there on their way to and from the coast. They knew that Livingstone was against their trade, and they hated him accordingly. Some, like Mohammed Bogharib, had sense enough to see his greatness, and to help him; but others, though they dared nothing to his face, did all they could behind his back to ruin his work and thwart his plans. Wherever they met him on his journeys, they would frighten, bully, or bribe his bearers to make them rebel. By telling the natives that Livingstone was really a slaver and a spy, they tried to make them refuse him food, guides, and canoes. There can be little doubt that they got hold of his messengers and destroyed his letters.

After a three months' rest at Ujiji, Livingstone felt well enough to set out again. Leaving orders for the new bearers from Zanzibar to come after him, he started with his old followers, and with the few stores he had been able to get together. In July 1869 he crossed Lake Tanganyika by canoe; then, striking to the north-west, he made his way on foot to Kabambaré, in the Manyema country. Here the River Luapula, flowing from Lakes Bangweolo and Moero, was known by the name of the Lualaba, and Livingstone hoped to explore it. Would the Lualaba prove to be the Nile or the Congo? That was the question he wanted to settle.

At Kabambaré the chief was called Moenékoos, a name meaning "Lord of the light-grey, red-tailed parrot": and he proved so friendly, that Livingstone rested in his village for ten days. Then, starting again in November, the explorer went westward, through Manyema, till he reached the River Luama, at a point ten miles from its junction with the great Lualaba.

The country through which they passed was wonderful in its beauty. Tall palms and forest timber crowded the valleys and clothed the hillsides to the skyline. Giant creepers, as thick as cables, were twisted round the massive trunks, or hung from limb to limb, and tree to tree, like the rigging of a ship. Lilies, orchids, clematis, and marigolds opened their rich colours to the light and poured their scent into the air; while all kinds of fruit clustered among the leaves. Gaudy parrots and other gay-feathered birds flashed about in the brilliant heat, while tribes of monkeys ran up the trunks, scampered along the branches, or swung themselves on the rope-like creepers. Sometimes a group of these would get together in a tree-top, and there they would chatter and grin about the news of the day, and the latest fashions of the monkey world. Sometimes they would jabber and grimace more earnestly, as though about monkey politics; and at times they lost their tempers and pelted each other with nuts and husks. Now and then one of them, either from annoyance or for sheer mischief, would take a shot at the travellers.

Villages were very frequent; and many of the natives kept goats, sheep, and fowls, and also had gardens of maize, bananas, and sugar-cane. Others were helpless and ignorant, even not knowing how to light a fire by twirling a pointed stick round and round inside a hole in a slab of wood.

The natives were not very friendly, for they believed that Livingstone was a slaver. Some of them said they were cannibals, and in order to frighten his bearers, showed them the skull of a "soko" or gorilla, which they had eaten. Livingstone found, however, that they never ate men; but often enticed a soko with a clump of bananas, and then speared him for food.

At the Luama, nothing could induce the natives to let Livingstone have a canoe with which to explore the Lualaba. He found out afterwards that even his own bearers tried to set the natives against him; for this, they thought, would force him to give up his journey and take them home. Indeed, the ceaseless worry of these worthless rascals did more to wear him out than all the toils of the journey.

Disappointed, but not beaten, Livingstone returned to Kabambaré, and stayed there for many months till the rainy season was over. Then, in June 1870, he started with only his three faithful followers, Susi, Chuma, and Gardner, and again made the attempt to explore the great river. But the natives, made unfriendly by the Arabs, refused to sell them food, and they soon grew ill and exhausted. Tramping through thorns on land, wading among sharp reeds and biting leeches in the swamps, their feet were cut and torn, and their wounds refused to heal. There was nothing to be done but to return to

Kabambaré: and this they did, reaching it so worn out and lamed, that they took three months to recover.

Livingstone was on the point of setting out a third time for the Lualaba, when he heard that his new bearers from Zanzibar were on their way towards him. He waited for them a long while, in the hope of letters, medicines, and stores, but his time and his hope were wasted. On 4th February 1871, ten worthless slaves came up with only one letter. Dozens of Livingstone's letters had been lost or destroyed, and their headman, Shereef, had stayed behind at Ujiji, spending all Livingstone's stores.

In less than a week the new bearers rebelled, and it took all Livingstone's powers to make them go forward. But in the end patience and extra wages persuaded them to go on, and at last Livingstone reached Nyangwé, on the Lualaba, on 29th March 1871. Here again the Arab slavers prevented him from getting canoes, so he could go no farther down the stream. But he heard that the Lualaba bore round so much to the westward, that he now thought it might prove to be the Congo.

While Livingstone was thinking what next he should do, there happened before his eyes a thing so utterly cruel, that it swept all else from his mind. He was walking in the native market, on the river bank at Nyangwé, watching the people exchanging their wares. The natives from the other shore came over in canoes every day to join in the marketing, and that morning about 1500 of them, mostly women, were present.

As Livingstone was moving away to his hut, he noticed that many of the Arabs were about with their rifles; and presently he heard shots in the market behind him. Turning sharply round, he saw that the Arabs were firing into the middle of the helpless crowd, who fled shrieking to their canoes. These were all jammed together in a small creek, and the natives struggled. and fell over each other in the effort to get them out.

Then a large party of Arabs, concealed near the creek, shot into the huddled mass, and the slaughter became terrible. Hundreds plunged into the river, and struck out for the other bank, while the murderers fired at them in the water. Some of the canoes were launched, and their crews escaped; others were over-loaded and upset. Many of the swimmers were picked up by their friends, but a large number were overcome by the strong current and sank. In all, about three or four hundred perished. One Arab took a canoe, and picked up some of the survivors, but the sight of Livingstone made him ashamed, and he gave them up to his care. Livingstone managed to save more than thirty, and he kept them safe till he was able to return them to their people. While the massacre was going on, the slaves from the Arab camp carried off all that had been left by the natives in the terror and tumult of their flight.

Livingstone at once made up his mind to return to Ujiji, and to send a report of this wicked outrage to England. He felt sure that his countrymen would now come to the rescue of this unhappy land, and he was right. His report of the massacre on the Lualaba was the deathblow to slavery in Central Africa, for it roused the whole English people. The British Government at once set to work, and, with the help of other nations, the slave trade was slowly but surely ended.

The tramp to Ujiji was full of hardship and danger. Livingstone was very ill, and in pain every step of the way, but the love of his duty carried him on. The cowardly Arab slavers knew his intention; and, though they dared not touch him themselves, they tried to persuade the tribes on his path to murder him. But most of the natives had now seen for themselves that Livingstone was not a slaver, and they answered that he was "the good one," and they would not kill him. Some of them, however, laid in ambush, and threw spears at him as he passed. He had several narrow escapes, and in one day a spear grazed his neck and another missed him by only a few inches.

At last, after trudging more than 500 miles in three months of daily suffering and risk, he crossed Tanganyika, and reached Ujiji at the end of October. He was worn out and at death's door, and now he found he was beggared. Shereef had made away with all his stores, and not an atom was left.

In this terrible need a friend came to him as suddenly as though dropped from the clouds. One day his followers heard that a white man was coming into Ujiji, and they rushed at once to tell their master. Livingstone went out to meet the stranger, and found, to his surprise, that a young journalist, H. M. Stanley, was coming to his relief, with a large caravan of stores.

Livingstone's work against the slave trade had made him so much liked in America, that an American, J. Gordon Bennet, had sent Stanley to find the great explorer, whom everybody thought to be lost.

This kind and generous act from another nation than his own, touched Livingstone very much, and he and Stanley became fast friends. Livingstone in return told all he knew about Africa, and Stanley was always grateful for this help when it became his turn to be a great explorer.

THE LAST JOURNEY

WHILE Livingstone and Stanley were together, they made a short journey to the north end of Tanganyika. They wanted to see if any river ran out of the lake towards the Nile; they found that a river, the Rusizi, flowed into the lake instead. Had they now crossed the Rusizi, and gone northwards, they would probably have settled the question of the Nile in a few months. But Stanley had to return, and Livingstone went with him.

Four months with Livingstone made Stanley as keen an explorer as his new friend. On their way back they talked much about the sources of the great rivers, and they both thought that the Lualaba might still run into the Nile. Had they only known it, Livingstone had already discovered enough to prove this quite impossible. At Nyangwé he had measured the height of the Lualaba above the sea-level, and had sent the measurements to England. Other people had sent measurements of the Nile as far as its course was known. Geographers at once saw from these that the Lualaba could never reach the Nile without running uphill. The Royal Geographical Society at once wrote this to Livingstone, and told him the Lualaba must be the Congo. But he never received the letter.

Stanley now tried to persuade his companion to go with him to England, but in vain. Livingstone had promised his friends at home to find the sources of the Nile, and he would not give up his promise. However, he returned with Stanley as far as Unyanyembé; for here he expected to find some stores from the British Government, who now also promised him a salary and a pension.

On their arrival they found that, as usual, the stores had been plundered and sold. Then Stanley, like a true comrade, shared all his supplies and spare clothes with Livingstone; and he also promised to try and find him fifty honest bearers in Zanzibar. On 14th March 1872 they parted in much sorrow, for they had grown to like each other greatly.

Livingstone waited at Unyanyembé till the end of August, when fifty-seven new bearers, chosen by Stanley, came up with supplies from Zanzibar. They were honest and faithful men; and, with them to help him, Livingstone started in good spirits for his last journey. He hoped to pass round the south of Lake Bangweolo, then westward of Lake Moero to the Lualaba; and then he would try and reach the Nile.

In six weeks they were at the south end of Tanganyika; and before January 1873 they had crossed the valley of the Chambezé, a river which runs into Bangweolo. They then worked round the south of that lake; but the rainy season broke early that year, and brought with it the usual floods and fever.

Livingstone was sixty years old, and the toil and suffering of the last seven years now told upon him terribly. He again fell very ill, and daily grew weaker. His faithful bearers, who loved him like a father, did all they could to take care of him, and carried him through mile after mile of marsh and flood. If these fine fellows had been with him six years ago, his work would long have been done. At times he began to think that he would not finish his task. "I shall never be able to play," he wrote to a friend who was resting after a life of hard work.

Day after day, in the pitiless rain, they toiled over the swamp-land, splashed through the flood, and forded swollen streams, sometimes up to the neck, with their burdens on their heads. A stretch of hard ground was a rarity, while food grew scarcer and scarcer, and fever got worse and worse. The bearers made a *kitanda*, or stretcher slung on a pole, for they saw that their Bwana (their master) was no longer able to sit up. There was no proper food for a sick man—for milk, the one thing most needed, was not to be had.

For four days Livingstone was too weak to write in his diary anything but the date. Then, on April 27th, he feebly scrawled, "Knocked up quite, and remain ... recover... Sent to buy milch goats." He still had pluck and hope of recovery, but his men had only grief. They scoured the country for miles around, but they could not get a single goat.

They saw the end must now come, and they pushed onward to higher ground, reaching the village of a chief called Chitambo on April 29th. Here their quick and skilful hands in a few hours built him a hut, and they laid him, in great pain, on a bed made of boughs and dried grass, covered with blankets. Susi tended him all next day, and at nightfall Majwara kept watch outside his master's door. In the dead of night Majwara came calling, "Come to Bwana, Susi, I am afraid."

Susi and some others crept reverently into the hut; and, by the flickering light of a candle, they saw the saviour of Central Africa dead on his knees at the bedside, with his hands to his face on the pillow.

It is a brave thing to die for one's fellow-men; it is also brave, and often far harder, to live for them. Livingstone did both. Indeed, the humble Blantyre mill-boy had done the noblest and highest thing that man can do; he had given his whole life to help God's less happy creatures. And this he had done, not for money nor for fame, but out of love for God and man.

In the grey dawn of May 1st, his faithful followers clustered round the camp fire to take counsel. They talked of their beloved Bwana, the master who never struck his bearers, and who nursed them like his own children when they fell sick. Had he not come from the far land of the great Queen, not to make slaves, like the Portuguese, but to set men free? Yes, he was a great white chief, and he must go home to the tombs of his fathers: that was certain, and they would see to it, or die. He had given some of his wisdom to Susi and Chuma, and they would be head-men.

Then Susi and Chuma made their plans. With reverent care they counted and packed all their master's things, and carried his body to an open spot near the village. Here some of them built a new hut, open to the sun, and began to embalm the body; while others made a stout wooden stockade around it. Outside all they built a circle of huts for themselves, and, night and day, they kept watch till the embalming was done.

They buried his heart beneath a large mvula-tree, and put up two posts and a cross-bar to mark the spot. A day of mourning was held, and all Chitambo's people, as is their custom, came with bows and spears; while the bearers fired volleys with their rifles. At last the body was wrapped, like a mummy, in bark and sailcloth, and lashed to a pole; and so the return journey was begun.

No praise is too high for the pluck and hardihood of this little band of faithful men. Once more they faced all the old risks and hardships of floods, fever, and want of food. They crossed the Luapula, and made for the south end of Tanganyika. Their great fear was about the ignorant fancies of the natives, who dislike a dead body passing through their villages. Often they had to pay toll, and once they were forced to fight. They came to a tribe of natives who had a large stockade, and also two villages close at hand. The people in the stockade had been drinking palm-wine, and the son of their chief was drunk. The chief might have proved friendly, but his son refused to let the travellers pass. He quickly forced on a quarrel, and his men began to shoot arrows.

Then Susi's party cleared the stockade of natives, and put their precious burden in one of the huts inside. Then, rifles in hand, they stormed the two villages, burning the huts and driving the people to their canoes. After this they lived on their spoil for a week in the stockade, till its owners came to make peace.

When they reached Unyanyembé, they met an expedition sent from England to search for Livingstone; and they learnt that another relief party had started up the Congo from the west coast. The officer at Unyanyembé wanted to bury the body at once. Susi and his men, however, stoutly refused to give up their purpose.

So the faithful band went on their work of love; and, after nine months on foot, reached the sea-coast at Bagamoyo, in February 1874. Here these black men of honour and ability handed over their master's body to the British Consul. All his property, too, was there, down to the last button.

Their task was done, and, with sad faces and heavy hearts, they were sent away.

Livingstone's body was carried to its grave in Westminster Abbey on 18th April 1874, by Oswell, Kirk, Young, Stanley, and others of his old friends. But the work of his noble spirit was not ended. All men hastened to do him honour, and many now began to do his bidding. He had once said that, if he could only bring about the end of the slave trade, he would count it "a far greater feat than the discovery of all the sources together."

The dirge over his grave acted on his country like a bugle-call to Africa. Other brave men pressed forward to carry on the work that the unselfish Scotch peasant lad had begun; and now slavery in Africa is all but ended. Livingstone sawed through the first slave-stick in the Shiré Valley: Gordon, Kitchener, Macdonald, and Wingate broke up the last strongholds of slavery on the Nile.

Livingstone just missed the Nile, but he found the source of the Congo, the third great river of the world. Stanley finished most of the pioneering that was left.

There is now a good road past the Murchison Cataracts, while Lake Nyassa floats two British gunboats and a fleet of trading steamers. The Universities' Mission, too, have their own steamer on the lake; and other missions also are hard at work on Livingstone's plans. Lake Tanganyika is joined by a road to Nyassa, and will soon be reached by railway from the Victoria Falls.

Besides this, the nations of Europe have divided Africa amongst themselves.

The British have taken the land of about thirty million blacks into their charge, and are trying to govern them justly. Many missionaries, all over the continent, are teaching the Africans how to make the best use of their lives. This is just what Livingstone hoped and worked for. He proved that gentleness and justice could make noble men, like Susi and his faithful band. Livingstone began this work of uplifting the black men, but he has left it to us to finish. Boys and girls will do well to think how they can help.

There are black men still in Africa whose faces light up with joy at Livingstone's name. They will answer and ask questions, in their quaint way, about the great man whom they called the Wise Heart and Healer of Men. "Yes, we loved him, and we served him too. Was he not our Bwana, who never struck his bearers? Of course we sent him back to the great White Queen. Did she not send him to Africa, not to get ivory and gold and slaves, like the Arabs and Portuguese, but to give a good message of wisdom, and to set men free? Have you many like him in your land? Ah, but his heart is still in Africa, under the mvula-tree at Chitambo's."

Printed in Great Britain
by Amazon